Fridfinnsson to produce a special edition of *Point d'ironie* to mark the occasion of this presentation of his work in London. We remain grateful, as always, to the Council of the Serpentine Gallery for their continued support, which is key to the realisation of exhibitions such as this one.

We would like to extend our thanks to the Ministry of Education, Science and Culture and the Ministry of Foreign Affairs in Iceland for their generous support, and we are very grateful to His Excellency Mr Sverrir Haukur Gunnlaugsson, Ambassador of Iceland to the UK, and to Vigdís Pálsdóttir, Cultural Attaché, for their kind assistance.

We would also like to acknowledge Pierre Huyghe and Philippe Parreno for their continued interest in and support of Fridfinnsson's work.

This publication features a number of engaging texts including a discussion with the artist, as well as texts by Olafur Eliasson, Snorri Sigfús Birgisson, composer, and Kitty Scott, Chief Curator, Serpentine Gallery. Herman Lelie and Stefania Bonelli have designed the catalogue and our thanks go to Melissa Larner for her editorial skills.

Finally, we are indebted to the entire teams at both institutions for their commitment to, and enthusiasm for, this project. At the Serpentine, particularly Kitty Scott; Mike Gaughan, Gallery Manager; Kathryn Rattee, Exhibition Organiser; and Sally Tallant, Head of Education and Public Programmes, and her team. At the Reykjavik Art Museum, Yean Fee Quay, Director of Exhibition Services; Soffía Karlsdóttir, Director of Public Relations and Development; and Ólöf K Sigurðardóttir, Director of Education.

Julia Peyton-Jones
Director, Serpentine Gallery and
Co-Director, Exhibitions & Programmes

Hans Ulrich Obrist
Co-Director, Exhibitions & Programmes and
Director, International Projects

Hafthor Yngvason
Director, Reykjavik Art Museum

4

Dropping by Jon Gunnar's 1965–1992

Hreinn Fridfinnsson

Serpentine Gallery

LISTASAFN REYKJAVÍKUR
REYKJAVIK ART MUSEUM

Directors' Foreword

Hreinn Fridfinnsson is one of Iceland's leading conceptual artists. His art is celebrated for its lyricism and stark poetry that transcends the often commonplace subjects and materials that the artist uses to create his work. Fridfinnsson's practice encompasses photography and drawing as well as installation. His works are linked, however, by a common sensibility and lightness of touch. Landscape and the natural world are central themes for Fridfinnsson and are the subject of several of his most significant works.

Fridfinnsson's work is well known in his native Iceland and elsewhere in Europe, where it has been featured in several group and solo exhibitions. His thoughtful and varied practice has been an important influence for a younger generation of artists, however it remains lesser known in Britain and the Serpentine Gallery is delighted to present the first ever solo exhibition of Hreinn Fridfinnsson's work in the UK.

A number of individuals were instrumental in realising this exhibition. First and foremost, we thank the artist for his generosity and attention to all aspects of his exhibition at the Serpentine and the Reykjavik Art Museum. Furthermore, we are grateful to him for kindly producing a Limited Edition Print, and for allowing the Gallery to benefit from its sale.

Artist Olafur Eliasson, co-designer, with Kjetil Thorsen, of the Serpentine Gallery Pavilion 2007, has initiated this exhibition with the Gallery and we thank him for the time and consideration he has given to the project as well as for contributing a stimulating text to this publication.

We are indebted also to the museums and private collectors who have agreed to share important works from their collections for this exhibition. The support of these lenders is crucial to the success of this project.

Our warm thanks also go to the artist's representatives: Börkur Arnarson of i8 Gallery, Reykjavik; Claes Nordenhake of Galerie Nordenhake, Berlin; Claudine Papillon of Galerie Claudine Papillon, Paris; and Ilona Anhava of Galerie Anhava, Helsinki. We remain most grateful to them for their invaluable assistance and advice throughout the planning stages of the exhibition.

We are thrilled to be working with agnès b on this exhibition and cannot thank Agnès enough for her vision and generosity in supporting the project. Moreover, we are delighted that she has collaborated with Hreinn

Five Gates for the South Wind (detail, facing page) 1971–72

Seven Times 1972

Attending 1973

Out of the Ordinary:
Hreinn Fridfinnsson's Experiential Experiments

The field of contemporary art continually brings forward the new, the known and the unknown. Sometimes the new comes in the form of young artists who are in the process of making a name and reputation for themselves through their work. At other times, the 'new' is relative and to be found in what is already there. Such is the case with Hreinn Fridfinnsson, who is well established within the contemporary art world of Iceland, where he was born, and Amsterdam, where he lives, but who is less well known to a wider audience. I first heard his name during a programming meeting with Serpentine Gallery Directors Julia Peyton-Jones and Hans Ulrich Obrist. We were meeting to discuss how we might synergistically programme the summer exhibition with respect to the Serpentine Gallery Pavilion 2007, designed by the well-known Danish/Icelandic artist Olafur Eliasson, in collaboration with the distinguished Norwegian architect Kjetil Thorsen, of the architectural practice Snøhetta. Obrist mentioned Fridfinnsson as a possibility, stating that this senior, Icelandic conceptual artist, who has been exhibiting since the early 1970s, has been a great inspiration to Eliasson, as well as to the French artist Philippe Parreno, among others.

I first met Fridfinnsson when he travelled to London for his initial meeting at the Serpentine Gallery. He is serious and gentle and his manner is straightforward and low-key; all of this is undercut by a self-deprecating sense of humour. Fridfinnsson set the pace. Slowly and deliberately, we reviewed a series of works from which we would later make a final selection. As he discussed his practice in depth, he introduced the central themes of his *oeuvre*, as well as his methods for making art. This brief essay will sketch the foundations of his practice and is followed by Hans Ulrich Obrist's interview with Fridfinnsson, where the artist speaks more intimately and directly about his history as well as specific works in the exhibition.

While reading about, and studying reproductions of, Fridfinnsson's work, a list of artists of similar sensibility came to mind: Bas Jan Ader, Carl Andre, Giovanni Anselmo, Giulio Paolini, Robert Smithson, Michael Heizer, Richard Long and James Turrell. Though distinctly different in their approaches, all of them were born, like Fridfinnsson, in the 1930s and 40s and the diversity of categories into which their work falls demonstrates the multiplicity of attitudes present in Fridfinnsson's work. It could be characterised as conceptual in the sense that it is ideas-driven, or as Arte Povera in its use of everyday materials; much of it might be considered stripped down or Minimalist, and the outdoor projects can be seen as examples of earthworks or land art.

A handful of works are exemplary. The conceptual work, *Substances*, composed of the text 'I have looked at the sea through my tears', 1973, evidences an emotional approach or perhaps a search for the ineffable and even beautiful. The earthwork, *House Project*, 1974, was built in a remote area of Iceland by Fridfinnsson and was based on a literary source describing an 'inside-out' dwelling, where the exterior was decorated with wallpaper, curtains and, of course, pictures. *House Project* was not meant to be a public work of art; rather, Fridfinnsson showed documentation of its construction in a Stockholm museum and hoped that walkers would come across the building itself by accident and then tell others about the experience. In fact, it was the artist's intention that *House Project* would become known as a rumour rather than a marked monument or sculpture. The simple sculptures *Sanctuary*, 1992–2007, and *Floor Piece*, 1992–2007, are made out of regular cardboard boxes and coloured paper, and at once they recall the ordinary materials characteristic of the Italian Arte Povera movement and the more durable metal sculptures of Donald Judd. Fridfinnsson makes use of precious materials too: *For Light, Shadow and Dust*, 1994, is a minimal wall work composed of a series of glass shelves, to which gold leaf has been applied, and its reflective surfaces make visible the ethereal, be it light, shadow or dust.

Not only does Fridfinnsson's practice span some of the most important contemporary movements of the last half of the previous century, but it also embraces many of the current ways of making art. The artist has exhibited photographs, drawings, paintings, sculptures and installations. He often incorporates readymades, or objects that come off the shelf. However, unlike many of his contemporaries, Fridfinnsson does not use a computer and he has yet to make a video available for public consumption. This gap in his activity speaks of an avoidance of the moving image, found in glowing screens and via projection that defines our contemporary digital existence.

Fridfinnsson grew up in a very different world: the unmediated magnificence of the Icelandic countryside, on a farm in the 1940s and 50s. He says it is impossible to separate himself from the landscape; it is in him, in his body and part of his psychological makeup.[1] The early experience of a vast unpopulated landscape and its accompanying rhythms is fundamental to understanding his work. Where many contemporary artists are fascinated by the speed and spectacle of the media, which could be seen to be accompanied by the loss of memory, Fridfinnsson exists in a parallel universe, where a more measured pace yields memories impossible to forget. This way of seeing, and the knowledge it produces, is familiar to those who find pleasure in natural surroundings. In such places, something big, and often ephemeral, pulls you in and holds you for a long time. Perhaps it is a pale grey sky changing to a foreboding black as a spring storm moves overhead, or maybe it is the ever-changing formation of a flock of white sheep, as seen on a sunny day against an emerald green hillside. Nothing in and of itself is remarkable about these scenes; they are part of the everyday flux in such environments. However, during our contemplation of these slow, considered moments, we sense the possibility that some modest discovery, or even something extraordinary, might be revealed within the ordinary. It is precisely this durational approach to looking, thinking and experiencing with which Fridfinnsson is engaged.

The artist's visual language is more complex, though. His vocabulary, often underscored by a delicate sense of humour, encompasses doubling, dreams, folklore, language games, mythology, pairing, perceptual tricks, reflections, and the supernatural. Through these means, Fridfinnsson, is searching for equivalence between one thing and another. Within this exhibition, for example, no one piece is more important or more central; instead, we find ourselves in the midst of a dispersed and non-hierarchical universe, where the wonder of a simple discovery is cause for celebration.

Kitty Scott

1 The author in conversation with the artist 28 May 2007

I dreamt that I was on the farm where
I was born and raised. My father (who
is dead) and I were working in the
homefield, collecting hay. We had a
horse there and a wagon, with which we
were going to transport the hay to the
stables. It was rather dark outside,
but quite warm. When we had loaded the
wagon, my father disappeared, but his
shadow was left behind and I knew that
I was to apply it to the hubs of the
wagon wheels to make them run more
smoothly. Then I was to attach the
wagon to the horse with strings made
of light which had shone down through
the sea. - Then I woke up.

Dream 1973

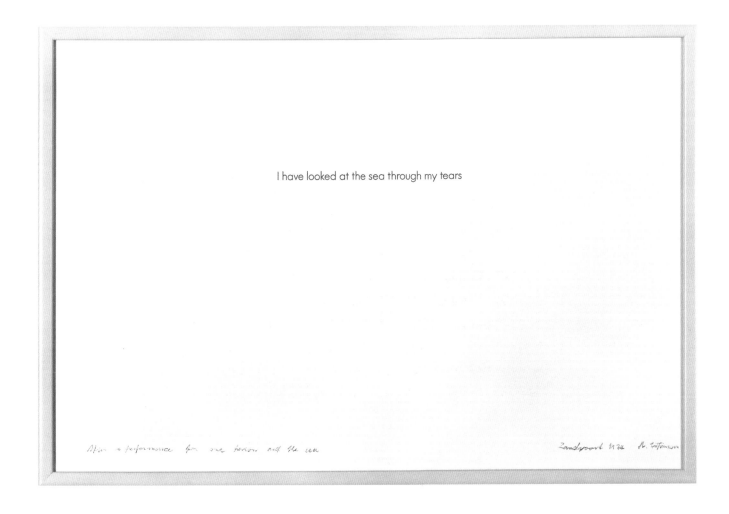

I have looked at the sea through my tears

After a performance for one person and the sea   Zandvoort 1974   M. Tuthmann

Substances 1973

House Project 1974

House Project 1974

World 1990–2007

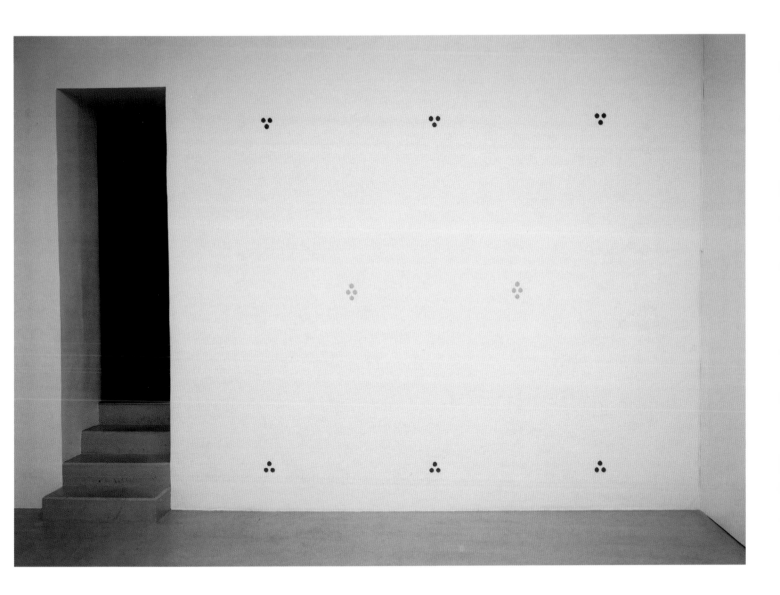

Landscape 1990

Having Hreinn in Mind

If Hreinn were everything, I would be everywhere.

If I were an artwork, I would like to be one of Hreinn's. Then I would enjoy not being selfish and, in particular, I would be pleased that what my being performed would be less about *being itself* and more about *being with*. Being with the world.

If I were a world, I would be the world that includes Hreinn's works. I would feel real – and this, partly through his works. My reality and my existence would be produced continuously both by the works and by everything else. With satisfaction, I would note that neither I, my being in the world, nor Hreinn's works, being his, would claim ownership of the area of exchange between us. The ideas we would exchange, and give way to, would fabricate a space; a field with the ability to include an ever-changing notion of time, and a distinct ability to perform reality 'as we go' without venturing down blind alleys made up of issues such as property and commodification. These ideas are good ideas. Good, because they are susceptible to change.

If I were an idea, I would like to be the kind that Hreinn's works unceasingly produce when being with the world, and I would slowly change everything and all things. When given access to temporality, ideas become intentions. If I were such an idea, I would evolve, not to become something better, but rather to unravel the fact that as an idea I would be able to have an impact on everything, to co-produce the world and develop my intentions. These intentions are not concepts about the world. Intentions are part of the world when they are allowed to breathe in time; our time.

If I were an idea, I would like to be of the kind that changes the world. Like a good discussion, I would be able to make a difference. The world, meaning all things and ideas gravitating towards the centre of the earth (as do Hreinn's works), needs differences. When ideas like the ones that his subtle works and the rest of the world exchange make differences, they constitute presence as a field rather than a dot on a line. We see these differences as we add time to our expectations while looking at Hreinn's artworks. Looking is taking part in the production of difference. Engagement has consequences, and the real is relative.

If Hreinn were everything, I would be everywhere. Everywhere as an endless field.

If I were a field, I would be the temporal field created by the fine-spun and generous relationships that Hreinn's works establish with the world. This field would be to my liking because it holds the potential for mapping time as a plane, not a line. In this particular field, the past, the present and the future may all be seen from everywhere else in the field. Regardless of my position, I seem able to orient myself equally well from within segments of the past and segments of my expected future. By thinking, I can relocate myself, and my view of the segments changes accordingly. The field is alive; it is here and now. Here with Hreinn's works and now in the world. There is space for evaluation, and by letting me reconsider the real, the field suggests dimensions in which Hreinn's subtleties perform the plural. Plural places and plural people.

If I were a language, I would like to be the one spoken by Hreinn's works. They go beyond a narrative and make a world instead of simply relating something about the world. With this language, they create a space of time not unlike the one I experience when I am in Iceland, in a city or a landscape. Here the light creates a subtle palette of grey hues, and roughly half of all daylight is in fact twilight. The Icelandic light shapes one's senses in a special way; it changes the way one perceives objects. The relation between objects and daylight or twilight calls for a constant re-composition of the objects and of ourselves.
If I were an object, I would be a subtle one, perhaps a quasi-object, continuously transformed by light.

If I were a text, I would like to be one sentence only.

Olafur Eliasson

First Window 1992

Floor Piece 1992–2007

For Light, Shadow and Dust 1994

Element of Doubt I 1997

Elsewhere 1998–2000

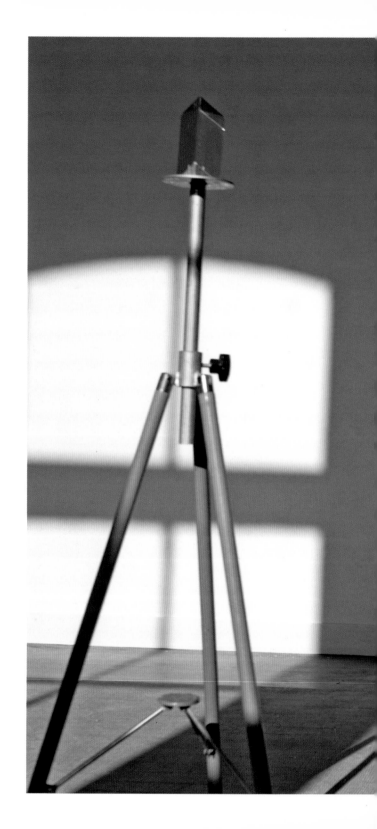

Untitled 2000

Mediterranean Impressions 1993

Music is present in the work of Hreinn Fridfinnsson. By this I do not mean specific musical references, like the burning harp in the piece *By the Roadside*. Nor do I wish to suggest that his art expresses emotions in a way similar to music. To clarify, I need to say a few words about music as a phenomenon.

It is the nature of music that it only exists when performed. As soon as a note is struck it begins to die and when a piece begins, it inevitably must end. The composer may strive to reinforce the structural aspects of his work – armed with rationality and concepts of form – but nothing can alter the fact that music is as transient as life itself; it is while it is, and then that's that.

Not so in art. A piece that one sees on Monday is exactly the same on Tuesday, a week after, or a year later. No matter how often a work of art is interpreted it can still be approached in its place, unbudged. And long after one stops looking, it still exists. Artwork occupies its physical space but music disappears just as it has been heard. Its essence is impermanence and it creates a reality that is unreal.

Music itself may seem insubstantial in the face of reality, but as we listen to a piece it is as if everything changes. When the final note has fallen silent, however, we see that such change is illusory. Reality is as it was although we may wonder about it while we are listening and even after a piece ends. All remains unchanged except perhaps us, ourselves.

Music is present in the work of Hreinn Fridfinnsson, and by this I mean that the essence of his art is the impermanence that comes with time's passing and that he shows us reality that is unreal. He shows us reality in an unexpected light but we know that nothing has changed. Except us, ourselves. We wonder…

Snorri Sigfús Birgisson
Composer

Suspended (detail) 2000

The Way We Were 2002

Hans Ulrich Obrist interview with Hreinn Fridfinnsson

HUO I thought it would be good to start with your piece of 1974 about secrets, which has become a legendary work; it's influenced so many artists all over the world. Could you tell me how the piece came about?

HF It exists only as an advertisement in a periodical. In the 1970s, when a group of us were running a small exhibition space in Amsterdam called the In-Out Centre, there was a little publication with a limited print-run called *Fandangos* that was run by a young artist couple in Maastricht. I contributed to it on two or three occasions and one of these was this advertisement. I announced that I was a collector of secrets and asked people to contact me and give me their secrets. But perhaps understandably, I didn't get a single one.

HUO So it didn't lead to an archive of secrets. Was the idea of the archive behind it?

HF Yes, or the notion of collecting and collectables. I was hoping that somebody would make contact, but I knew it was highly unlikely. People don't normally entrust a stranger with their secrets. The work was playing with the nature of the secret – I, as a collector of secrets, would not want to trade or pass them around since then they would cease to exist.

HUO Somebody could still call you today with their secret.

HF Absolutely. It isn't a dead thing at all. I could still present it.

HUO In the 1960s and 70s, there was a tendency towards what Lucy Lippard called 'the dematerialisation of the object', and most of these dematerialised artworks were related to documents. Your project about secrets seems to have pushed that one step further: so many people have told me about this work that it almost functions like a rumour.

HF Yes, that's what people have told me. I don't remember being conscious of that aspect at the time.

HUO Another of your works that has been talked about a lot by young artists is your 'inside-out house', *House Project*, of 1974. Can you tell me about the genesis of this piece?

HF Again, it's mainly a text work: it's presented as the documentation of the event, as evidence that the house was built, and it belongs to a museum in Stockholm. The idea originated in an old Icelandic book from the early 20th century. A certain gentleman in a village – he was considered to be quite an eccentric – decided to build a new house for himself. He started in the traditional manner with a shell constructed from wood and corrugated iron. But instead of putting the iron on the outside, he put it on the inside. According to the story, it was a decorative purpose that lay behind this idea, because he wanted to use wallpaper, which was a novelty, and he thought it would make sense to put it on the outside where more people could enjoy it. This was for me just a fantastic thing: a house turned inside-out. Then I realised that it had a meaning. You could claim that such a house turns the world inside-out. So that was the drive to build a similar little house. I stumbled across an ideal site in a lava area not far from Reykjavik and we built it quickly. One of the basic factors of the project was that the building itself wasn't a sculpture for people to visit. The piece was presented as documentation.

HUO So it was more about the story-telling than about the actual experience?

HF Yes. It was never intended as a sculptural piece. And then it was just left where we built it. But an important part of it is that once in a while ramblers walking around in this area came across it. Little by little, I started hearing stories from people who'd come across this funny house in this area. That was the intention: that it shouldn't be advertised that there was an art piece there. This was exactly what I was after.

HUO Again, it's almost like a secret.

HF In a way, yes. And then the rumour spreads. It stayed there, I heard, in quite a reasonable condition for 20 years, and it's only in the last 10 years that it's deteriorated; there's nothing left of it now except some stuff lying around.

HUO You had discussions with Jessica Morgan at the Icelandic Festival about rebuilding it, didn't you?

HF She suggested I should rebuild it. At first I agreed, but then I realised that this was an exhibition project, and the duration would be only three

From the construction of House Project 1974

From Mont Sainte Victoire 1998

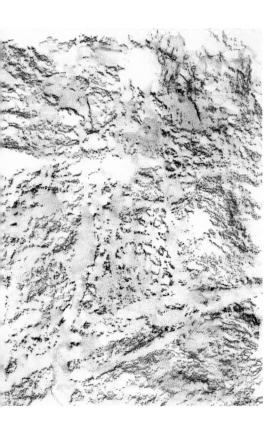

or four months. To rebuild this house and then to take it down would turn it into a theatre set of sorts. And there's something about it that you can't exactly repeat. So I don't think it will happen. But I would like to realise something on that same site one day.

HUO So you made something else for the Icelandic Art Festival. You did an installation in the north of Iceland.

HF I made an alternative suggestion that's based on the original house project and it's meant, in a way, as a kind of taking leave of it. Gallery Slunkariki, where Jessica finally decided to put my work, is a small gallery in the village of Isafjördur, which has been run very successfully for a great number of years. The feature of the Gallery that stuck in my mind was that in the floor is a trapdoor, which opened on a stairway to the basement. I wanted to lift this lid or do something with it. Last spring, the lid was opened and three more sides with mirrored surfaces were added, so that there was a mirror box with a stairway instead of a bottom. It opened the space up; it made it quite large. You could see into every corner of the basement, just from walking around this mirrored box. The opening of the stairway turned into a field or grid, which extended in all directions. On the walls of the gallery space upstairs I had some frottage drawings; I placed drawing paper directly on the wall and I rubbed over it with a pencil so that all the remains of whatever had been done to this wall came through. So upstairs it's a very clean, classical sort of a gallery space, but in the middle you have a basement that contains all kinds of stuff with all kinds of histories.

Of course, it also has a kind of architectural dimension to it. And another strand of the house project is that when I had a retrospective show at Domaine de Kerguéhennec centre d'art contemporain, I was invited to do something in the sculpture park. Again, what I put forward was based on this house, but it proposes another way to deal with it, and that's to turn it back into a normal house with things inside it, but it would be a closed house that you couldn't enter; you could only peep through the windows. That project is now in progress, and if all goes well it will be realised this year. And then I think the *House Project* will be finished.

HUO Many of your projects start with a text as the central element. To what extent is writing and story-telling important for you, particularly Icelandic sagas?

HF There are a lot of stories, narrative pieces often accompanied by photo presentations. My first solo show took place here in Amsterdam in 1971, and that was a group of 12 text photos with the title *Sacred and Enchanted Places*. I collected material about the places, and then I visited and photographed them. They were all special places in nature – a little piece of a stone or a part of a meadow or a hill – or buildings and farmhouses in the countryside. But they were all places that had spells on them. For example, you can't mow the grass or move the stone because then something bad will happen.

HUO And the form of the work is basically two photographs left and right and a text in the middle.

HF Yes. The reason for the two photographs is that one is taken from a distance so that one gets a sense of the surroundings; the other is a close-up of the spot that's had a spell cast on it. The stories and their sources are very varied; some were from books and publications, some given to me by people. I travelled around to collect stories about places of this sort. I found some places in Reykjavik through a specialist in these kinds of stories and myths and traditions.

HUO What was his name?

HF Arni Ola. He wrote some literature, but mainly he was a story collector and he was very precise, presenting these very old stories as a sort of history. I phoned him up and talked to him about a certain stone in Reykjavik, which is now quite close to the centre, but when these particular events took place, it was outside the city. So it was very good to learn about it from such a source. I took good care that the stories were as accurate as possible. And these narrative pieces are still going on. Story-telling is very important for me; it's just in my nature.

HUO You yourself have written beautiful texts, for example *Dream* from 1973. Is writing a daily practice? Have you ever written novels?

HF Not at all, no. I hardly write at all any more. I used to a bit. I tried writing some texts, but never anything approaching a book or a poem. *Dream* was simply written down. I've done two 'dreams' so far. There was another one some years later for a booklet published in conjunction with one of the Centre Pompidou's opening exhibitions, *Ca va? Ca va?*,

Enchanted rock in Reykjavik

In the year 1934, a man called Thorbjörn bought a small piece of land in Ármúli which was then quite a long way from Reykjavik. This lot was very rocky and Thorbjörn got four or five men from the town to clear it. The rocks were to be taken to the harbour where they would be used for the extension of the harbour. One of the rocks was situated in the south part of the lot. It was quite large, but very low, and from beneath it came a spring. The workers drilled a hole into it and it was to be blown up the following day. During the night, Thorbjörn dreamt that a man came to him. This man appeared to be very distressed and asked why his home was not being left in peace. Thorbjörn asks where his home is and the man replies that it is the rock in the south part of the lot. He adds that if it is disturbed further there will be grave consequences. Thorbjörn decides to let the stone be and carries out his plan of building a poultry farm. In 1940, a group of bakers bought the poultry farm, with the lot, from Thorbjörn. They employed a man called Tönsberg as manager. He was told the story about the rock, but decided all the same to have the lot cleared and made into a field. Work was begun and, on May 20th, 1942, two holes were drilled into the rock. It was to be blown up within a few days. However, a sudden change then occured in the egg production at the poultry farm. Thönberg's records note this change as follows:

    May 21 - 343 eggs
    May 22 - 320 eggs
    May 23 - 312 eggs
    May 24 - 235 eggs

On May 25th the rock was to be blown up, but for some reason there was a delay:

    May 26 - 120 eggs
    May 27 - 80 eggs
    May 28 - 47 eggs
    May 29 - 20 eggs
    May 30 -   8 eggs
    May 31 - no eggs

Tönsberg brought in a veterinarian to examine the hens and sent a sample of the fodder to the University lab. On the following days, no eggs were found. Tönsberg now remembered Thorbjörn's story of the rock and began to consider it. It took him two weeks, however, to make a decision and during that period, May 31st to June 14th, there was not one egg laid. Finally, five eggs were found. From that day on the laying of eggs increased gradually until it was normal again. Since the time of these events, the city of Reykjavik has grown so that the rock is now almost in the center of town, where it stands undisturbed to this day.

Sacred and Enchanted Places 1972

curated by Jean-Hubert Martin. There were four of us in the show, and a box of four small booklets was published instead of a catalogue. Then there were some more text works and stories in catalogues. There were also some stories from Icelandic folklore published in artists' magazines in the early 1970s.

HUO Like many other Icelandic artists, you went into exile; you went to Amsterdam. Could you talk a little bit about this notion of travel in relation to your work?

HF The term 'exile' is far too dramatic – I wasn't running away when I went abroad. I was just exploring what was beyond my immediate horizon. A youngster with a leaning towards art, who was born and raised in an isolated place, gets this idea of the world outside: whatever is outside is just attractive. This is the same theme that goes through the sagas. To go away is the thing, but not to escape; that's probably also there, but it's of much lesser weight than the simple desire to go to new places. It just happened and it was one coincidence after another. My first trip abroad was to London, in 1963. I spent some time there on and off throughout the 1960s. These trips were quite aimless; it was just, 'Why not go there?' And then in the late 1960s, I was in Rome. I was there in the historic year 1968. Then I just drifted to Holland because my then wife got a position here with a dance company. It's just life that brings one to the places where one sometimes spends an unbelievably long time. It wasn't my intention to stay in Holland forever.

HUO There's still quite a strong presence of Icelandic places in your work. It's a discussion we've been having with Olafur Eliasson, who said that even though he's been away from Iceland for many years, it's almost magnetic; he keeps coming back and the landscape of Iceland continues to nurture him. Is that also the case for you?

HF In the 1970s, I used all kinds of material of Icelandic origin, but that didn't have to do with being homesick or missing the place; I just found folklore fitting as material to be transformed into contemporary art. Lately, I've made some photographic works in Iceland, but the specific location didn't play a big role. I think this pull was stronger in the 1970s.

HUO What was your relation to the whole conceptual art movement during the 1960s and early 70s? Obviously, both London and Amsterdam were central to that movement at the time. Were there any dialogues with other artists that were particularly important for you?

HF There were not that many in London. In Rome – strangely, because the art world there was quite dull in those days: it was all film, film, film – there were a few like-minded individuals and that was stimulating and inspiring; we had very good exchanges. But in Amsterdam, it was completely different. There weren't that many galleries, just a few memorable ones, like the tiny Art & Project, which was tremendously important. And the Stedelijk Museum was very lively, very active and a good cultural institute in the 1970s. And there were all the museums as well, of course. But there was a constant flow of people; much of the time we had people staying with us, sleeping on the floor. They came from all over the place. So the 1970s was a time when there was a lot of exchange, a lot of contact and movement and openness in this place.

HUO What about earlier influences? Another thread throughout your work is geometric abstraction, in terms of the way in which you arrange your photographs in geometric patterns, or the squares in a work like *Principle and Temptation*, 1998–91. Is that triggered by early-20th-century utopias?

HF *Principle and Temptation* is a photographic work that has the structure of a golden rectangle; when divided into progressively smaller squares, the resulting radii, the so-called golden spiral, appears, which corresponds to the Fibonacci sequence of numbers. This is not a geometric abstraction designed by me; it's an existing formula. I also added a colour range to the image. In one of the smaller squares, there's an inserted figurative image, a photo of a shadow play with hands creating an image of a bird. But geometric abstraction was my first big love in the 1950s, and I'm extremely fond of this kind of art. I guess there's an influence there.

HUO How did you come into contact with geometric abstraction at the time? There were geometric painters in Iceland in the 1950s like Karl Kvaran, the father of Gunnar Kvaran. Was this important?

HF Absolutely. Of course, for a kid, everything is important; everything is interesting and everything is instantly imitated. A lot of the Icelandic abstract artists came from, or had some connection with, the Parisian school and also painted figuratively. I came into contact with this art through black and white images in the newspaper because I was living in the countryside. I didn't see a painting until I left. I saw images by people like Thorvaldur Skúlason, Karl Kvaran, Hördur Ágústsson and Svavar Gudnason. There were a lot of painters making Abstract Expressionist work in those days, but I was more drawn to the geometric side rather than Abstract Expressionism.

HUO Of which Kvaran was the great one.

HF Kvaran, yes, and all these slightly older artists. Some of his works were at that time important influences. And then, little by little, I came across other people through publications from Reykjavik. Quite some time before I went to art school in 1958, I'd seen radical, important works by Mondrian. This was a particular type of composition that I must admit I made hundreds of imitations of. 'This is the end-point in art', I thought to myself at the time, and I thought that nothing needed to be added to it. These were very great, enlightening moments, because life in the countryside was basically isolation from the visual arts; it simply wasn't there, except for the occasional photo in the newspaper. Malevich came later; I didn't see any works by Malevich, or the Russians, until I'd gone to the city. This was the dominating influence that shaped my way of looking at things in this early period.

HUO The object has always had a presence in your work, but at the same time, it's surrounded by doubt. If you think about the house, for example, it's not really about the object. In the 1980s, you started to do large works that were more object-orientated, but you soon dropped this idea. Your objects aren't monolithic, they're not heavy, they don't occupy space; many are more like triggers – they're more like what Michel Serre would call 'quasi-objects'.

HF I'm really at a loss as to what to say about objects. I can't remember the last time I constructed something. I don't feel attracted to making constructions. For example, I was one of several artists invited to make a proposal for a public artwork in a large new building for the water and energy companies, the height of which is almost 40 metres. Each artist was to choose a particular space in the building. In the search for an idea for this particular space, I began investigating, along with Kristinn E Hrafnsson, a friend and colleague who was helping me, the history of Foucault's Pendulum. I quickly saw that there was no way that I could make any sculpture for this location that would be more interesting than Foucault's Pendulum. This is, of course, an object that belongs to the history of physics; in the end, it was built by a physicist and a team of people. I was very happy to be a part of this process, but I haven't constructed an object for a long time.

HUO You see no reason to add any more objects to the world?

HF Not at the moment. This view, of course, has undergone many changes throughout the time that I've been working as an artist. The disappearance, the absence of the object, came very naturally in the Conceptual era. It wasn't something that one had to work hard on. But still the object in my work never disappeared. An object can be a wonderful thing, and objects came back with force in the beginning of the 1980s; that was the spirit of the time. I think I'd just had enough of these immaterial ideas floating around. The constructions I made in the 1980s were the result of a strange kind of 'must'. You find yourself in a particular time and you have to work through it, and suddenly you're out of it and that's a great feeling. But there are a few of these object works that I can defend. They weren't all bad, I think.

HUO No, on the contrary, they're very important. Which would you single out in particular?

HF There was a work you might have seen in Reykjavik: *A Folded Star*. It was done for an exhibition in Gallerie Bama in 1983 or 84. But I think the idea had been with me for some time – it was just one of those things that's there, but there hadn't been any need to realise it until that time. It's a pentagram that when folded makes a pentagon.

HUO What would be other key object works for you?

HF In the 1980s, I worked very hard on a group of sculptural works and some of these survive, but quite a few never took off. I thought really hard about these pieces; there was a lot of logic to me in them. They're not really key works, but they're the only survivors from a period that wasn't very fruitful.

HUO This is interesting; you're basically saying that the period where you produced more has, paradoxically, been the least fruitful.

HF Yes. Most of the time, the things that turn out to have been of more substance, or have opened up possibilities, are the result of what you might call luck: they happen to you; you stumble onto them or they're accidents; things go wrong and then some part of it turns out to be exactly the right thing. But then, I'd never say that I'm against a certain form or I wouldn't want to make a massive work; it's nothing like that. It's not a decision. These things are never planned; they just happen to you. You travel back and forth and circle around things and you realise you're circling around a core of similar things.

HUO Very often you revisit previous images. How is this organised? Is it systematic, through an archive, or is it random?

HF It is absolutely not systematic: this return to older works is just something that happens. The process is like memory. I have something that's unfinished, a certain idea or piece from 20 or 30 years ago, and it invites me to take it one step further, or to add a little twist to it. I don't have an archive, I just have memories.

HUO And how do those memories pop up? For example with *Drawing a Tiger* of 1971, you revisited an old photograph of you as a child drawing a tiger and then sort of re-enacted it.

HF I wouldn't use the term 're-enacting'. It was just using an old image to make a work. I came across this old photo of me, taken in 1952, in the family album. I just got an idea to repeat that act in a new situation, in a new location, and after all that time had elapsed in between. What really sparked the work was that there was a photo of this kid sitting outside in the garden drawing something and it was very clear, very visible, what the kid was drawing. It was very inviting to draw it again. Reworking older works does take place now and then. For example, *So Far* of 1974 was remade in 2002. The story and the image are in the catalogue from Kerguéhennec.

HUO Also in the Kerguéhennec catalogue there's a series of photographs called *Sheep and Horses of my Nephew*, 2001. Is this another kind of archive?

HF I don't think it has anything to do with archive. It had often crossed my mind during my visits to the family farm to make a photo-work of

Drawing a Tiger 1971

the sheep in the meadows, but I didn't want to make the photos myself, so I asked the farmer, my nephew, to do it. These are his photographs: the composition is made with his eye. There are these interesting formations of the movement of a flock of sheep, depending on the land's topography, but there's a big difference between my nephew's aesthetic sense and my own. A farmer looks at his sheep differently from the way I would, so that influences the composition of these photographs. There's also an earlier photo work that was taken by my nephew, called *First Window*, 1992, a photograph of a window in the house where I was born and raised, and this was given the subtitle *Homage to Marcel Duchamp*.

HUO You gave him instructions?

HF Yes, I just asked him to find the window and take a picture. The result was very good.

HUO This open instruction idea features in many of your works. You participated in the *Do It* book of artists' instructions and it's there in many of your text pieces and photographs. Could you talk a little bit about the role of the instruction?

HF It's about giving a very basic idea to somebody else and trusting the outcome. Your collaborator's occupation will influence the outcome. If that person happens to be an artist, then it would be a particular kind of work. An artist has a tendency to go towards a certain style or towards something that ties ideas down one way or another; but when the idea is given away to others – just a little spark will do – the results are often agreeable and have, at least in my mind, an airy quality.

HUO That's like what John Cage said when he talked about his chance music.

HF Yes. I've always found that approach attractive and rewarding.

HUO Would you refer to a work like *Sanctuary*, 1992, and some of the other pieces you've made with boxes, as 'altered readymades'?

HF I use both readymades and prefabricated materials. The idea is to alter them slightly to achieve a transformation of the material into a work. It's a minimal interference. The boxes could be called altered

Sheep and Horses of my Nephew 2001

readymades because sheets of fluorescent paper were inserted inside in order to change the tint of the light coming from the outside. One box was mounted on the wall; with the bottom slightly open, you could see that it had a bluish tint on the inside that was different from the light inside the box and on the wall around it. *A Palace*, 1990, is a good example of my use of the readymade: this piece is made of chicken wire that was cut down into sections. It grows on the wall by adding up squared numbers from 1 to 12.

HUO It's systematic?

HF That one is systematic and in a way a little architectural.

HUO In terms of the readymade, I was also wondering about your very early piece called *Dropping by Jon Gunnar's* from 1965.

HF This piece, made from a door, was done for the 1965 exhibition in Reykjavik that later became known as *SÚM 1*. I got the door from Jón Gunnar Árnason, a friend and colleague who was also participating in the show. He was rebuilding his home, and this door was lying around and I asked him if I could take it home. I simply found it a beautiful object. I took it to the studio where I lived. I looked at it for many, many weeks, because I had no idea what to do with it. Then, in a fit of doubt, I broke it and painted the pieces, which in a way is a violent act, but there was no violence involved in getting it from my friend. Some people asked, 'Did you break in to Jón Gunnar's house and was that the reason for this piece?' But in fact the process was peaceful.

HUO This notion of the found object interests me in terms of your sonic work, because you also use found sounds. For example, *Movement/ Déplacement* from 1999 uses the sound of cars passing by.

HF The 'sounds' in *Movement* are not actually sounds that I experienced. They're described in the novel *Drei Kameraden* (*Three Comrades*) by the German writer Erich Maria Remarque. The book, in Icelandic translation, had been given to my father. It was a favourite of mine when I was a kid. I had it in my studio, which was totally clogged up after almost 10 years of working there. In about 2000, when I had to leave the studio, I had a photo taken of myself there, reading the book. I read a page where a character describes the sound of a car passing. I stopped in the middle of the page, and then I moved to a new studio (which was completely empty) and finished the page there. There's no symbolic meaning about moving from one studio to another. I just wanted to make a work out of the experience, and the book happened to be there. I hadn't opened it since I was a kid.

HUO And what about *Song/Chanson*, 1992–2000?

HF The *Song* pieces are made by photographing the screen of an oscilloscope, which is activated by singing. It was made in stereo, so I got a loop that twists and dances around. I wanted an image made as directly as possible with sound. I knew that incredible things can be done with technology today, but this was probably the most primitive form of an image made by sound.

HUO It's almost like a machine for images.

HF Yes. It's a machine for images. There's a relationship between this work and a work I made around the same time with images from a kaleidoscope, where the multitude of images indicates the potential for going on and on, and the impossibility of the same image ever being repeated.

HUO Which brings us to the question of time. In the late 1980s, early 1990s, your work was very influential, because of the way it emphasised time, which was a rarely used medium in art history – works like *Seven Times*, 1972, and *After a While*, 1976, for example. Could one say that time is your medium?

HF It's something that recurs a lot in various ways – sometimes in a very straightforward sense and sometimes in a more complex form. Time, or notions of time, are always compelling. I read what comes my way about physics and mathematics, but I read as one who's uninitiated. It's very difficult to get your mind around these concepts, but it is possible to read about them with fascination. My interest in the essence of time is serious, but my dealing with time is not knowledge-based; it's more exploratory and feeling-based.

HUO What about *After a While*? In that work the idea of time is particularly strong.

 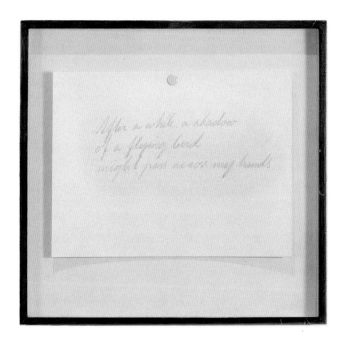

After a While 1976

HF It's a diptych. On the left is a photo of my work table on which lies a piece of paper with something written on it. The image on the right is a small piece of paper with a sentence written on it; it's the paper itself, transported out of the photographic image. It's a movement/time work.

HUO And you've recently been involved in an exhibition about time.

HF In 2005 a gallery in Brussels requested work with a time theme. I made an installation consisting of a huge Möbius strip and two digital codes from a round-trip baggage-claim ticket. I chose them because I find them visually pleasing, and, of course, they're loaded with information. In addition, there's a little meteorite and one tiny curl of pencil shaving, each on a pedestal. These details were picked from the planned house project in France.

HUO So appropriately, we finish by returning full circle to the inside-out house. Many thanks Hreinn for the interview.

Untitled 2006

The Fall

It was the still, frosty, almost cloudless morning of February 12, 1947, in Eastern Siberia, when at 10:38 local time a bolide appeared in the sky, clearly visible in the full sunlight. It initially looked like a bright star, but soon turned into a dazzling fireball, which became slightly elongated. The bolide rapidly crossed the sky from north to south, leaving behind it a boiling dusty trail of meteoroid particles. Then it passed out of sight behind the hills in the Sikhote-Alin mountains.

During the last visible segment of its trajectory, the bolide split into several parts. Several minutes after the bolide's glow disappeared, local inhabitants heard loud bangs like explosions or a cannonade. Then followed thunder that rolled far over the taiga and resounded over and over in the Sikhote-Alin ridge.

The most intense phenomena were reported by witnesses in villages situated along the meteoroid's trajectory. They told of doors swung open, windows broken and plaster falling down during the fall. Flames burst out of furnaces, ashes and smoldering brands flew out. Horses neighed, cows mooed, they broke loose and dashed around. Dogs rushed undercover yelping or ran away to the forest.

Almost all witnesses reported that the bolide's flight lasted only 4-5 seconds. It was observed across an area more than 600 km in diameter. The giant trail of dust and smoke remained in the sky for the rest of the day. Gradually it became twisted due to strong air currents in the upper atmosphere. The trail disappeared only at sunset.

An artist named Medvedev witnessed the meteoroid flight and painted the scene right away. Ten years later, in 1957, his painting was reproduced on a Soviet postal stamp.

Within two days, the location of the meteorite's fall had been determined by pilots who saw clearly marked fresh craters amidst untouched snow. Soon afterwards, a group of geologists arrived from Khabarovsk. They examined the craters and holes and gathered the first specimens of the meteorite's iron.

Thorsteinn Surtr dreamed he was awake but everyone else was asleep

Thorsteinn Surtr dreamed he was awake but everyone
else was asleep; then he dreamed he fell asleep and
everyone else woke up
Book of Icelanders Ari the Learned, c1125 2002

then he dreamed he fell asleep and everyone else woke up.

List of works in exhibition

Dropping by Jon Gunnar's
1965–1992
Wood and paint (reconstruction)
215 x 75 cm
Courtesy of the artist and
i8 Gallery, Reykjavik

Drawing a Tiger 1971
Photographs (diptych)
Each: 57.7 x 51.7 cm
Courtesy of the artist and
i8 Gallery, Reykjavik

**Five Gates for the South
Wind** 1971–72
Black and white photographs
and text
Each: 15.5 x 20.5 cm
Centre Georges Pompidou,
Musée National d'Art Moderne,
Paris

**Sacred and Enchanted
Places** 1972
Photograph, text on paper
52 x 72 cm
Claes Nordenhake

Seven Times 1972
Seven black and white
photographs
Each: 29.8 x 20.3 cm
Courtesy of the artist, i8 Gallery,
Reykjavik, and Galerie
Nordenhake Berlin/Stockholm

Attending 1973
Two colour photographs
Each: 55.5 x 70 cm
Courtesy of the artist and
i8 Gallery, Reykjavik

Dream 1973
Framed text on paper
20 x 20 cm
Courtesy of the artist and
i8 Gallery, Reykjavik

Substances 1973
Text, glass
40 x 60 cm
Courtesy of the artist and
i8 Gallery, Reykjavik

House Project 1974
16 colour photographs and
typewritten text
Each: 33 x 40 cm
Courtesy of the artist

So Far 1974–2002
Photographs (diptych)
Each: 53 x 53 cm
Michael Krichman and
Carmen Cuenca

After a While 1976
Framed photograph and text
on paper
Each: 29.5 x 30.6 cm
Collection Per Sandven

Landscape 1990
PlayDoh, 26 elements
Dimensions variable
Courtesy of the artist and
Galerie Nordenhake
Berlin/Stockholm

A Palace 1990
Chicken wire
433 x 500 cm
Courtesy of the artist and
i8 Gallery, Reykjavik

Summer Nights 1990
Coloured paper
Each: 80 cm high
Courtesy of the artist and
i8 Gallery, Reykjavik

World 1990–2007
Clay, 26 elements
Dimensions variable
Courtesy of the artist and
Galerie Nordenhake
Berlin/Stockholm

First Window 1992
Colour photograph
100 x 75 cm
Collection Anne-Marie and
Marc Robelin

Floor Piece 1992–2007
Fluorescent paper, bookbinding
material, cardboard box
Dimensions variable
Collection of Petur Arason and
Ragna Robertsdottir

Sanctuary 1992–2007
Cardboard box, paper
67 x 46 x 32 cm
Collection of Petur Arason and
Ragna Robertsdottir

Mediterranean Impressions
1993
Photographs
6 x 7 cm
Courtesy of the artist and
i8 Gallery, Reykjavik

For Light, Shadow and Dust
1994
Gold leaf, glass
Four shelves, each:
0.8 x 80 x 15 cm
Collection FRAC Bretagne

Ephemeral Painting 1995
Mirages bowl, mini-painting
25 x 25 x 7 cm (bowl),
3 x 3 x 3 cm (mini-painting)
Courtesy of the artist and
i8 Gallery, Reykjavik

Element of Doubt I 1997
Mdf, wood
20 x 20 x 10 cm
Collection of Petur Arason and
Ragna Robertsdottir

Element of Doubt II 1997
Mdf, wood
20 x 20 x 10 cm
Collection of Petur Arason and
Ragna Robertsdottir

From Mont Sainte Victoire
1998
Graphite on paper
Each: 36.7 x 28.1 cm
Courtesy of the artist and
i8 Gallery, Reykjavik

Elsewhere 1998–2000
Ink jet print
124 x 186.4 cm
Henna and Pertti Niemistö
Collection of Contemporary
Art/Hämeenlinna Art Museum,
Finland

Placement 1999–2007
Glass paint on glass (diptych)
Each: 22 x 22 cm
Courtesy of the artist and
i8 Gallery, Reykjavik

Untitled 1999–2007
Crystals
Dimensions variable
Courtesy of the artist and
i8 Gallery, Reykjavik

Untitled 2000
Colour photograph
124 x 190 cm
The Museum of Contemporary
Art Kiasma, Helsinki

Drops 2000–2007
Crystals
Each drop: 7.5 cm
Courtesy of the artist and
i8 Gallery, Reykjavik

Suspended 2000
Stirring sticks
Dimensions variable
Courtesy of the artist and
i8 Gallery, Reykjavik

**Sheep and Horses of my
Nephew** 2001
Colour photographs
Each: 19.5 x 29.4 cm
Courtesy of the artist and
i8 Gallery, Reykjavik

Jar 2002
Polished steel, glass
25 x 200 x 125 cm
Michael Krichman and
Carmen Cuenca

Jars 2002
Polished steel, glass
100 x 125 x 125 cm
Michael Krichman and
Carmen Cuenca

The Way We Were 2002
Four black and white
photographs
Each: 4 x 26.7 x 33.2 cm
Courtesy of the artist and
i8 Gallery, Reykjavik

**Thorsteinn Surtr dreamed
he was awake but everyone
else was asleep; then he
dreamed he fell asleep and
everyone else woke up
Book of Icelanders
Ari the Learned, c1125** 2002
Vinyl
10 x 520 cm
Courtesy of the artist

Beauty Marks 2004
Velvet
Dimensions variable
Courtesy of the artist

Pair 2004/2005
Mirror with silver wooden frame,
shoe
48 x 57 cm (mirror), overall
dimensions variable
Courtesy of the artist and
i8 Gallery, Reykjavik

Pair 2004/2005
Mirror with silver wooden frame,
shoe
40 x 50 x 100 cm
Galerie Nordenhake
Berlin/Stockholm

Untitled 2006
Meteorite, vinyl letters
258 x 245 cm
Courtesy of the artist

**Fishing Fly (Thunder and
Lightning)** 2007
Glass and fishing fly
22 x 22 cm
Courtesy of the artist and
i8 Gallery, Reykjavik

Fishing Fly (Nymph) 2007
Glass and fishing fly
22 x 22 cm
Courtesy of the artist and
i8 Gallery, Reykjavik

Fishing Fly (Mayfly) 2007
Glass and fishing fly
22 x 22 cm
Courtesy of the artist and
i8 Gallery, Reykjavik

Summer Nights 1990

Biography

Hreinn Fridfinnsson
Born 1943 in Dalir, Iceland
Lives in Amsterdam

Solo Exhibitions
2006
Sudsudvestur, Keflavik, Iceland
Galerie Claudine Papillon, Paris

2005
Reykjavik Arts Festival, Gallery Slunkaríki,
Ísafjörður, Iceland

2004
Galerie Nordenhake, Berlin

2003
i8 Gallery, Reykjavik
Safn, Reykjavik

2002
Domaine de Kerguéhennec, centre d´art
contemporain, Bignan, France
Kyoto Art Center, Kyoto
Galerie Papillon-Fiat

2001
Ljósaklif, Hafnarfjördur, Iceland
E 541 Art House, Iceland

2000
Ars Fennica, Waïnö Aaltonen Museum
of Art, Turku, Finland; Hämeenlinna Art
Museum
Galerie Papillon-Fiat, Paris

1999
Edition Camomille, Brussels
Galerie Anhava, Helsinki
i8 Gallery, Reykjavik
Galerie Alexandra Von Scholz, Berlin

1998
Gallery 20m², Reykjavik
Gallery Fiskurinn, Reykjavik
Collection, Another Place, Amsterdam

1997
Galerie Claudine Papillon, Paris
Gallery Corridor, Reykjavik

1996
Gallery Alexandra von Scholz, Berlin
Gallery Sólon Islandus, Reykjavik
Galerie Nordenhake, Stockholm

1995
Galerie Nordenhake, Stockholm
i8 Gallery, Reykjavik
Galleri Riis, Oslo

1994
Galerie Claudine Papillon, Paris
Galerie Camille von Scholz, Brussels
Galerie Anhava, Helsinki
Galleri Riis, Oslo
The Living Art Museum, Reykjavik
Ultima Thule, Amsterdam

1993
Venice Biennale, Icelandic Pavilion, Italy
National Gallery of Iceland, Reykjavik

1992
Galerie Nordenhake, Stockholm
Rhythms in Space, ICA, Amsterdam

1991
Gallery Van Gelder, Amsterdam

1990
Galerie Claudine Papillon, Paris
Reykjavik Arts Festival, Gallery II,
Reykjavik

1989
Galerie Nordenhake, Stockholm
Gallery Slunkaríki, Ísafjörður, Iceland

1988
Nordic Arts Centre, Galleria Augusta,
Helsinki
Kunstnernes Hus, Oslo

1987
Forum, Galerie Bama, Zürich
Gallery Suzanne Biederberg, Amsterdam
Le Magasin/Centre National d'Art
Contemporain, Grenoble

1986
Galerie Bama, Paris

1985
Suzanne Biederberg Gallery, Amsterdam

1984
Galerie Bama, Paris

1979
Galerie Helen Van der Meij, Amsterdam
Galerie Bama, Paris

1977
Gallery Sudurgata 7, Reykjavik
Galerie Seriaal, Amsterdam

1976
Galerie Gaetan, Geneva
Galerie Elsa Von Honolulu, Ghent,
Belgium

1974
Gallery SÚM, Reykjavik

1973
Gallery Fignal, Amsterdam
In-Out Centre, Amsterdam

1972
In-Out Centre, Amsterdam

1971
Gallery 845, Amsterdam
Gallery Fignal, Haarlem, Netherlands
Gallery Balderich, Mönchengladbach,
Germany

Group Exhibitions
2007
Ad mynda ord, Hoffmannsgallery, Reykjavik

2006
Wintery Cold, Gallery Van Gelder,
Amsterdam
Chers Amis, Domaine de Kerguéhennec,
Centre d'art contemporain, Bignan, France
EMMA (opening exhibition), Espoo, Finland
Northern Images, Hoffmannsgallery,
Reykjavik

2005
Horizontal Memories (Water Event, Astrup
Fearnley Museum of Modern Art, Oslo)
Tivoli, Hveragerdi, Iceland
Polyfoni, Suomenlinna, Helsinki

2004
Éblouissement, Jeu de Paume, Paris
Les mémes et méme quelques autres,
Galerie Claudine Papillon, Paris
Handlungsanweisung, Kunsthalle Wien,
Vienna
Where do we go from here, Tanya
Bonakdar Gallery, New York
Ars Fennica, State Russian Museum,
St. Petersburg
Ars Fennica, Aboa Vetus Ars Nova, Turku,
Finland
Out of Place, Galerie Nordenhake, Berlin
Do it, e-flux

2001
Somewhere over the rainbow, FRAC
Haute Normandie, France

2000
Carnegie Art Award 2000, Helsinki, Oslo,
Goteborg, Copenhagen, Stockholm,
Reykjavik
Norden, Kunsthalle Wien, Vienna
Amateur/Eldsjäl, Goteburg Art Museum,
Goteborg
Interplay, Contemporary Art Museum, Oslo
Árátta, Listasafn Kópavogs, Iceland

In the Mirror of Space & Time, Ásmundarsalur, Reykjavik
64°N - 20° V, Galerie Nordenhake, Stockholm
Museum of Earth, Warsaw
Azerty, un avécédaire autour des collections du FRAC Limousin, Centre Georges Pompidou, Paris

1999
00, Gallery Van Gelder, Amsterdam
Dularfulli gardurinn, Ásmundarsalur, Reykjavik
Museum of Foreign Art, Riga
Natures Mortes, Galerie Papillon-Fiat, Paris

1998
Losse werken, rake klappen, Gallery van Gelder, Amsterdam
Look me in the eyes, Gallery Van Gelder, Amsterdam

1997
De Verbouwing, de Verhuizing & de Verandering, Gallery Van Gelder, Amsterdam
Tekeningen, Gallery Maria Chailloux, Amsterdam

1996
Landscape, Reykjavik Municipal Art Museum, Reykjavik
Dix ans de Création à Marseille, CIRVA, Musée de la Charité, Marseille
Maisons-Cerveaux, La Ferme du Buisson, Noisiel, France

1995
Maisons-Cerveaux, FRAC Champagne-Ardenne, Reims, France
Collection, FRAC Limousin, Limoges, France
Tekeningen & tekeningen, Gallery Van Gelder, Amsterdam
Pas pour la galerie, Galerie Camille Von Scholz, Brussels

1994
Wanås 94, Wanås, Sweden

1993
Edities & unica, Gallery Van Gelder, Amsterdam
Reconsidered images, Gallery Van Gelder, Amsterdam

1992
Gallery Van der Berge, Goes, Holland
Ijsland – Island, Zeeuws Museum, Middelburg, Holland
Il paesaggio Culturale, Palazzo delle Esposizioni, Rome
Artscape Nordland, Hattfjelldal, Norway

1991
Six logos around the carpet, Gallery Van Gelder, Amsterdam
Kunst Europa 1991 – Island, Kölnischer Kunstverein, Cologne
Galerie Claudine Papillon, Paris
They see the light, Gallery van Gelder, Amsterdam
Ruhrfestspiele, Recklinghausen, Germany

1990
Utopies, Grand Palais, Paris
Ruhrfestspiele, European Workshop, Kunsthalle Recklinghausen, Germany
New Nordic Art, The Central House of Artists, Moscow
Achilles de kwetsbare plek, Kasteel Groeneveld, Baarn, Holland
The End of the Century, The Museum for Crafts, Moscow
The Nordic 60s, Upheaval and Confrontation, National Gallery of Iceland, Reykjavik; Nordic Art Centre, Helsinki

1989
Galerie Claudine Papillon, Paris
SÚM, 1965–1972, Reykjavik Municipal Art Museum, Reykjavik
Borealis 4, Nordic Art Centre, Helsinki; Louisiana Museum of Modern Art, Humlebaek, Denmark
Suzanne Biederberg Gallery, Amsterdam
Utopies 89 – L'Europe des Créateurs, Grand Palais, Paris
Many Pearls for a Line, Gallery Van Gelder, Amsterdam

1988
Aldarspegill, National Gallery of Iceland, Reykjavik
Nýlistasafnid 10 ára, The Living Art Museum, Reykjavik

1986
Nordanad, Musée des arts décoratifs, Paris; Malmö Konsthall, Malmö, Sweden

1984
10 gestir á Listahátíd, Reykjavik Municipal Art Museum, Reykjavik

1983
ARS '83, Ateneum Art Museum, Helsinki

1982
Einkaheimar – Personal Worlds, The Living Art Museum, Reykjavik
Sleeping Beauty – Art Now, Scandinavia Today, Solomon R. Guggenheim Museum, New York;
The Port of History Museum, Philadelphia;
Municipal Art Gallery, Los Angeles

1981
Aspects de l'art d'aujourd'hui 1970 – 80, Musée d'art et d'histoire, Geneva

1978
Elva moderna isländska konstnärer, Malmö Konsthall, Malmö, Sweden
Personal Worlds – Reality as Metaphor, Stedelijk Museum, Amsterdam

1977
Ça va?, Ça va?, Centre Georges Pompidou, Paris

1975
Kunstmuseum, Lucerne, Switzerland
Galerie Waalkens, Finsterwolde, Holland

1974
Frans Hals Museum, Haarlem, Netherlands
H²0, St. Nicolaj Kirke, Copenhagen
Driemans-tentoonstelling, Gallerie t'Hoogt, Utrecht, Netherlands

1973
8ᵉ Biennale de Paris, Musée d'art moderne de la Ville de Paris, Paris

1972
SÚM á Listahátíd í, Gallery SÚM, Reykjavik
Communications, Gallery Inhibodress, Sydney

1971
SÚM IV, Museum Fodor, Amsterdam

1969
SÚM III, Gallery SÚM, Reykjavik

1967
SUM '67, Laugardalshöll, Reykjavik

1966
Den Nordiske Ungdomsbiennale for Bildende Kunst, Louisiana Museum of Modern Art, Humlebaek, Denmark

1965
SÚM I, Ásmundarsalur, Reykjavik

Permanent Installations
2007
Domaine de Kerguéhennec, Centre d'art contemporain, Sculpture Park, Bignan, France

2006
Ísafjörður Collage, Iceland

2004
Reykjavik Energy, Iceland

1993
Artscape Nordland, Hattfjelldal, Norway

1982
Amsterdam City Hall

Peder Lund
Aniz Manji
Andrew and Jacqueline Martin
Vincent and Elizabeth Meyer
Mr Donald Moore
Gregor Muir
Paul and Alison Myners
Cornelia Pallavicini
Katherine Priestley and David
 Pitblado
Ivan and Marina Ritossa
Hugo Rittson-Thomas
Kadee Robbins
David Roberts
Lily Safra
Alan and Joan Smith
Lord Edward Spencer-Churchill
Mr and Mrs David Stevenson
Siri Stolt-Nielsen
Ian and Mercedes Stoutzker
Laura and Barry Townsley
Melissa Ulfane
Dr Vera Vucelic
Peter Wheeler and Pascale
 Revert
Mr Bruce Wilpon and Mrs Yuki
 Oshima-Wilpon
Mr Samer Younis and Mrs Rana
 Sadik
Poju and Anita Zabludowicz
Riccardo Zacconi

Future Contemporaries

Committee
Matthew Dipple and Christopher
 Taylor
Tim Franks
Liz Kabler
Dan Macmillan
Bobby Molavi
Jake Parkinson-Smith
Stan Stalnaker
Cristina Revert
Marcus Waley-Cohen
Jonathan Wood

Members
Alia Al-Senussi
The A Team Foundation
Laura Bartlett
James and Felicia Brocklebank
William Burlington
Mr and Mrs Gaurav Burman
Lucy Chadwick
Cristina Colomar
Sophie Eynon
Flora Fairbairn
Moritz Fried
Philip Godsal

Colin M Hall
Edward Hanson
Camilla Johnson-Hill
Jeff Holland
Leila Khazaneh
Jack Kirkland
Arianne Levene
Marina Marini
James Morse
Samira Parkinson-Smith
Andrew Pirrie
Rebecca Richwhite
David Risley
Miss Naiki Rossell Pérez Correa
Isabelle Nowak and Torsten
 Winkler
Lucy Wood

Benefactors
Heinz and Simone Ackermans
Shane Akeroyd
Mishari Al-Bader
Marie-Claire Baroness von
 Alvensleben
Dr and Mrs Paul Armstrong
Max Alexander and Anna
 Bateson
Archeus
Mrs Bernard Asher
Alan and Charlotte Artus
Pedro C de Azambuja
Laurie Benson
Anne Best
Roger and Beverley Bevan
Lavinia Calza Beveridge
David and Janice Blackburn
Anthony and Gisela Bloom
Mr and Mrs John Botts
Marcus Boyle
Vanessa Branson
Michael and Pauline Brennan
Nick and Paulette Brittain
Mrs Conchita Broomfield
Benjamin Brown
Mr and Mrs Charles Brown
Ossi and Paul Burger
John and Susan Burns
Mr and Mrs Philip Byrne
Jonathan and Vanessa Cameron
Andrew Cecil
Monkey Chambers
Azia Chatila
Shirin Christoffersen
Mr Giuseppe and the late
 Mrs Alexandra Ciardi
Dr and Mrs David Cohen
Louise-Anne Comeau
Carole and Neville Conrad
Alexander Corcoran
Pilar Corrias and Adam Prideaux

Gul Coskun
Joan Curci
Linda and Ronald F Daitz
Helen and Colin David
Paul Davies
Ellynne Dec and Andrea Prat
Neil Duckworth
J Randolph and Denise Dumas
Adrienne Dumas
Mike Fairbrass
Mr and Mrs Mark Fenwick
Stephanie Ferrario
John Ferreira
Ruth Finch
Hako and Dorte Graf von
 Finckenstein
Harry and Ruth Fitzgibbons
David and Jane Fletcher
Bruce and Janet Flohr
Robert Forrest
Eric and Louise Franck
Honor Fraser
James Freedman and Anna Kissin
Lady Deedam Gaborit
Tatiana Gertik
Zak and Candida Gertler
Leonardo and Alessia Giangreco
Hugh Gibson
David Gill
Mr and Mrs John Gordon
Dimitri J Goulandris
Francesco Grana and Simona
 Fantinelli
Linda and Richard Grosse
The Bryan Guinness Charitable
 Trust
Philip Gumuchdjian
Sascha Hackel and Marcus Bury
Abel G Halpern and Helen
 Chung-Halpern
Roderick and Jenny Hall
Louise Hallett
Mr and Mrs Rupert Hambro
Mr and Mrs Antony Harbour
Susan Harris
Maria and Stratis Hatzistefanis
Mr and Mrs Rick Hayward
Thomas Healy and Fred
 Hochberg
Alison Henry
Michael and Sarah Hewett
Mrs Samantha Heyworth
Mrs Juliette Hopkins
Mrs Martha Hummer-Bradley
Montague Hurst Charitable Trust
Mr Michael and Lady Miranda
 Hutchinson
Iraj and Eva Ispahani
Nicola Jacobs and Tony
 Schlesinger

Mrs Christine Johnston
Susie Jubb
Howard and Linda Karshan
Jennifer Kersis
Malcolm King
James and Clare Kirkman
Tim and Dominique Kirkman
Mr and Mrs Charles Kirwan-
 Taylor
Herbert and Sybil Kretzmer
Britt Lintner
Barbara Lloyd and Judy Collins
Sotiris TF Lyritzis
Steve and Fran Magee
Mr Otto Julius Maier and Mrs
 Michèle Claudel-Maier
Claude Mandel and Maggie
 Mechlinski
Cat Martin
Mr and Mrs Stephen Mather
Viviane and James Mayor
Alexandra Meyers
Warren and Victoria Miro
Susan and Claus Moehlmann
Jen Moores
Gillian Mosely
Richard Nagy and Caroline
 Schmidt
Andrei Navrozov
Angela Nikolakopoulou
Dalit Nuttall
Georgia Oetker
Sandra and Stephan Olajide
Tamiko Onozawa
Mr and Mrs Nicholas Oppenheim
Linda Pace
Desmond Page and Asun
 Gelardin
Maureen Paley
Dominic Palfreyman
Midge and Simon Palley
Kathrine Palmer
Andrew and Jane Partridge
Julia Peyton-Jones
George and Carolyn Pincus
Lauren Papadopoulos Prakke
Victoria Preston
Sophie Price
Mathew Prichard
Max Reed
Michael Rich
John and Jill Ritblat
Bruce and Shadi Ritchie
Kasia Robinski
Kimberley Robson-Ortiz
 Foundation
Jacqueline and Nicholas Roe
Victoria, Lady de Rothschild
James Roundell and Bona
 Montagu

Rolf and Maryam Sachs
Nigel and Annette Sacks
Michael and Julia Samuel
Ronnie and Vidal Sassoon
Joana and Henrik Schliemann
Glenn Scott Wright
The Selvaag Family
Nick Simou and Julie Gatland
Mr and Mrs Jean-Marc Spitalier
Bina and Philippe von
 Stauffenberg
Tanya and David Steyn
Simone and Robert Suss
Emma Tennant and Tim Owens
The Thames Wharf Charity
Christian and Sarah von
 Thun-Hohenstein
Britt Tidelius
Suzanne Togna
Emily Tsingou
JP Ujobai
Ashley and Lisa Unwin
David and Emma Verey
Darren J Walker
Audrey Wallrock
Offer Waterman
Rajan and Wanda Watumull
Pierre and Ziba de Weck
Daniel and Cecilia Weiner
Alannah Weston
Helen Ytuarte White
Robin Wight and Anastasia
 Alexander
Martha and David Winfield
Mr and Mrs M Wolridge
Chad Wollen and Sian Davies
Nabil N Zaouk
Andrzej and Jill Zarzycki

And Patrons, Future Contemporaries and Benefactors who
wish to remain anonymous

International Media Partner
FORTUNE

This catalogue is produced to accompany *Hreinn Fridfinnsson*
at the Serpentine Gallery, London, 17 July – 2 September 2007
and at the Reykjavik Art Museum, 10 November 2007 – 27 January 2008

Prepared and published by the Serpentine Gallery, London

Julia Peyton-Jones
Director, Serpentine Gallery and Co-Director Exhibitions & Programmes

Hans Ulrich Obrist
Co-Director Exhibitions & Programmes, and Director of International Projects

Exhibition curated by Kitty Scott, Chief Curator
Organised by Kathryn Rattee, Exhibition Organiser
Catalogue edited by Melissa Larner
Designed by Herman Lelie and Stefania Bonelli, London
Produced by fandg.co.uk
Printed in England by Dexter

Serpentine Gallery
Kensington Gardens
London W2 3XA
T +44 (0)20 7402 6075   F +44 (0)20 7402 4103
www.serpentinegallery.org

Photographic credits
pp20 – 22, 57: Gerhard Kassner, Berlin; p23: Jan O Almerén, Stockholm;
p33: Laurent Lecat

ISBN 978-1-905190-16-4 (Serpentine Gallery, London)
ISBN 978-3-86560-308-1 (Verlag der Buchhandlung Walther König)

Distribution:

Europe
Buchhandlung Walther König
Ehrenstr. 4
D – 50672 Köln
T +49 (0)221 205 96 53   F +49 (0)221 205 96 60
order@buchhandlung-walther-koenig.de

UK & Eire
Cornerhouse Publications
70 Oxford Street, GB-Manchester M1 5NH
T +44 (0)161 200 15 03   F +44 (0)161 200 15 04
suzanne.davies@cornerhouse.org

Outside Europe
D.A.P./Distributed Art Publishers, Inc., New York
155 Sixth Avenue, New York, NY 10013
T +1 212-627-1999   F +1 212-627-94847

Sponsored by

agnès b.

With kind assistance from

The Ministry of
Education, Science and
Culture of Iceland

The Ministry of Foreign
Affairs of Iceland

Embassy of Iceland, London

Serpentine Gallery

LISTASAFN REYKJAVÍKUR
REYKJAVIK ART MUSEUM

THE
ROYAL
PARKS

City of Westminster